Weekend Fun

Let's Go to a
Science Center

By Mary Hill

Welcome
Books™

Children's Press®
A Division of Scholastic Inc.
New York / Toronto / London / Auckland / Sydney
Mexico City / New Delhi / Hong Kong
Danbury, Connecticut

Photo Credits: Cover © Dave G. Houser/Corbis; all other images by Maura B. McConnell
Contributing Editors: Shira Laskin and Jennifer Silate
Book Design: Michael DeLisio

Library of Congress Cataloging-in-Publication Data

Hill, Mary, 1977-
    Let's go to a science center / by Mary Hill.
    p. cm.—(Weekend fun)
    Includes index.
    Summary: Describes the experiences of a young girl and her mother when
    they visit a science center.
    ISBN 0-516-23996-1 (lib. bdg.)—ISBN 0-516-25920-2 (pbk.)
    1. Science museums—Juvenile literature. [1. Science museums. 2.
    Museums.] I. Title. II. Series.

Q105.A1.H55 2004
507'.4—dc22

                     2003012003

1 2 3 4 5 6 7 8 9 10 R 13 12 11 10 09 08 07 06 05 04

Contents

My name is Jane.

Today, my mom and I are going to a **science center**.

N THE MANDELL CENTER

5

There are many things to do at the science center.

First, I want to learn about **electricity**.

ELECTRICITY
HALL

PECO

ELECTRICITY

7

There is a kind of electricity in this **machine**.

ELECTRICITY
HALL
→PECO

r side of the lightning tube. What happens?

*The spinning metals jumping
toward one knot or strikes to
— glowing streams of lightning
during thunderstorms.
— lightning is much more
than these streamers,
extremely dangerous.*

9

We also learn about **Earth**.

I learn about the rocks and water on Earth's **surface**.

I learn about **weather**, too.

This machine shows how weather works.

Tornado

13

We also learn about the human body.

14

15

I learn how my heart works.

Back to the Heart

The pulmonary vein carries oxygen-rich blood (red) from your lungs back to your heart.

17

Next, we learn about space.

I look through a big **telescope**.

It helps me see things in space.

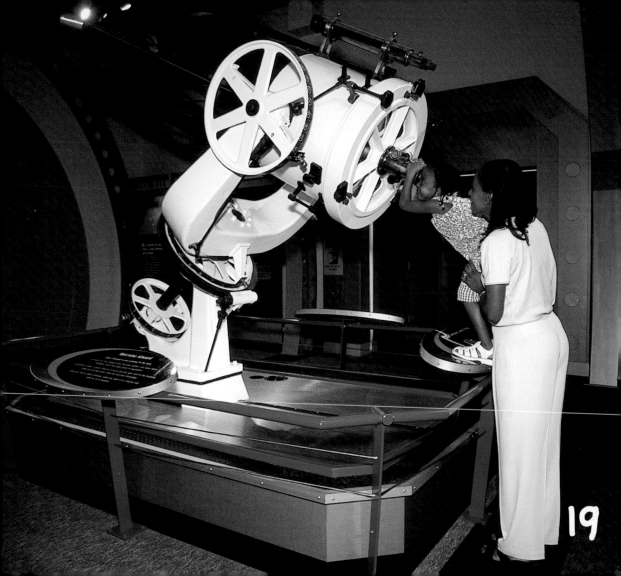

19

I learned a lot at the science center!

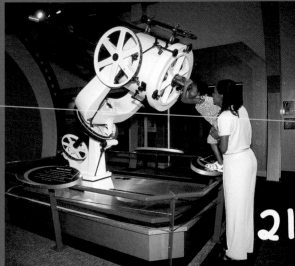

21

New Words

Earth (**urth**) the planet on which we live

electricity (i-lek-**triss**-uht-ee) a kind of energy that is used in many ways

machine (muh-**sheen**) something with moving parts that is used to do a job

science center (**sye**-uhnss **sen**-tur) a place where people go to learn about Earth and other planets, stars, electricity, oceans, the weather, animals, plants, the human body, and other natural things

surface (**sur**-fiss) the outside or outermost layer of something, such as Earth

telescope (**tel**-uh-skope) a tool that makes distant objects seem larger and closer

weather (**weth**-uhr) how hot or cold it is outside and what it is like outside in other ways

To Find Out More

Books
Don't Know Much about Space
by Kenneth C. Davis
HarperCollins Children's Book Group

More Nature in Your Backyard
by Susan Lang
Millbrook Press

Web Site
ARS: Sci4Kids
http://www.ars.usda.gov/is/kids/
This Web site has lots of science information. Learn about plants, animals, space, and the many things scientists are doing around the world.

Index

About the Author

Mary Hill has written many books for children. For fun on the weekends, she likes to go sailing.

Reading Consultants

Kris Flynn, Coordinator, Small School District Literacy, The San Diego County Office of Education

Shelly Forys, Certified Reading Recovery Specialist, W.J. Zahnow Elementary School, Waterloo, IL

Paulette Mansell, Certified Reading Recovery Specialist, and Early Literacy Consultant, TX